A Cold Place

Written by Jo Windsor

Rigby

This penguin is in a cold place.

3

This polar bear is in a cold place.

5

This bird is
in a cold place.

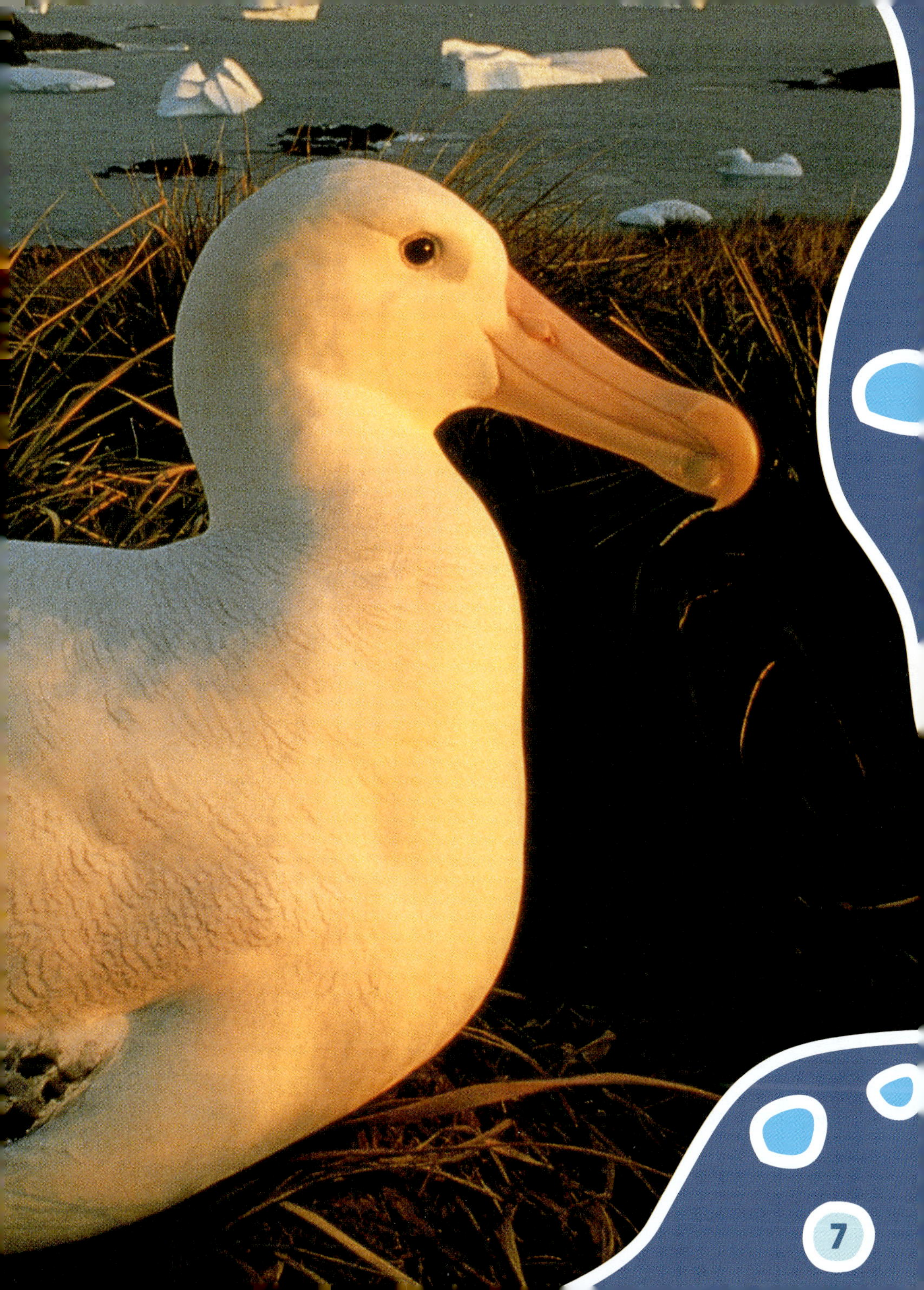

This seal is
in a cold place.

9

This whale is in a cold place.

11

This man is
in a cold place, too.

13

14

Index

bird 6-7

man 12-13

penguin 2-3

polar bear 4-5

seal 8-9

whale 10-11

Guide Notes

Title: A Cold Place
Stage: Emergent – Magenta
Genre: Nonfiction (Expository)
Approach: Guided Reading
Processes: Thinking Critically, Exploring Language, Processing Information
Written and Visual Focus: Photographs (static images), Index
Word Count: 42

FORMING THE FOUNDATION

Tell the children that this book is about a man and different animals that live in cold places. Talk to them about what is on the front cover. Read the title and the author.
Focus the children's attention on the index and talk about what they will find out about in this book.
"Walk" through the book, focusing on the photographs and talk about the man and the different animals, and where they live.

Read the text together.

THINKING CRITICALLY

(sample questions)

After the reading
- How do you think the polar bear keeps warm?
- Look at page 12/13. How do you know this is a cold place?

EXPLORING LANGUAGE

(ideas for selection)

Terminology
Title, cover, author, photographs

Vocabulary
Interest words: penguin, place, polar bear, seal, whale
High-frequency words: this, is, in, a
Positional word: in